Kregger's Antiques
916 - 969 - 3242

Kregger's Antiques
916 - 969 - 3242

Ludwig (Ludvik)
MOSER
King of Glass

A Treasure Chest of Photographs
and History

by
Mural K. Charon

Photography by John C. Mareska, M.D.

Fully illustrated in color,
including glass colors, signatures,
dimensions, and designs.

DEDICATION

I dedicate this book to my five children, Tom, Terry, William, Cheryl and James, for their interest and confidence shown in me, and Dr. John Mareska whose urging made me write words on pages and put pages in book form.

ACKNOWLEDGEMENTS

The author expresses her warmest appreciation and thanks all those persons who have shared valuable information and helped to make this book informative and useful. I am especially indebted to the following:

Mr. and Mrs. Paul Neuhauser
Mr. and Mrs. James Tally
Mr. and Mrs. Loyd Southworth
Mr. and Mrs. Vane Porter
Dr. and Mrs. John Mareska

TABLE OF CONTENTS

FOREWORD

At least eighteen years ago, my late husband, George, and I purchased our first collection of glass by a man named Moser. The fine quality of his wares and its exceptional decoration, spurred us on to do constant research on the man behind such remarkable objects of lasting beauty.

We have purchased hundreds of pieces of Moser glass from private collections throughout the United States, Canada and the French provinces. These examples have permitted us to conduct an intensive study of both the glass and the decorations used on it. The author will attempt to enlighten the collector to the various shapes and decorations that Moser employed, thus lessening the possibilities of mistaken attributions. As an art glass dealer, avid collector and teacher of art glass seminars, I urge collectors to know and appreciate glass and then collect it for its beauty and quality, not its signatures.

This book was especially written to give rightful credit to Ludvik Moser and his descendants. I am also fulfilling a promise to the many collectors of this glass who have been waiting over ten years for me to write this book; I feel that I owe them this knowledge.

Mural K. Charon
Grand Rapids, Michigan

Mural K. Charon has been a collector and a dealer in antique glass for many years. She and her late husband, George, were students of art glass and studied the iridescent glass of Tiffany, Steuben and Durand who manufactured glass in America. Over the past 20 years she has researched and collected Moser Glass. Mrs. Charon inherited the interest in fine glass from her mother and is now known as an authority on art glass and particularly on Moser Glass. She has lectured to the American Glass Club of Washington, Detroit clubs, New Orleans groups, at the Chrysler Museum of Norfolk, Virginia and in many other places. With this background, we believe she is the best qualified person to write this book.

-Milton M. Ferguson, publisher

LIST OF PROMINENT PERSONALITIES/ OWNERS OF MOSER GLASS SETS

MAHARANI - 4400 P.O. SET

Maharajah Surrendra Singh of Allrajpour
King Mohamed V of Marocco
President Sukarno of Indonesia
Government of Rumania
Sonja Henie, American actress
Crown Prince Asfa Wossen of Ethiopia

ROYAL - 9000 P.O. SET

King Edward VII of Great Britain
Queen Alexandra of Great Britain
King Haakon VII of Norway
Sultan Abdul Hamid of Turkey
President Celal Bayar of Turkey
President Assgeirsson of Iceland
Maharajah of Baroda
Maharajah of Navanagar
Diplomatic missions of Czechoslovakia
National Assembly of Guinea
Embassy of Phillippines, Canberra

COPENHAGEN - 9900 O.P. SET

Shah Mohamed Reza Pahlavi of Iran
King Amanullah of Afghanistan
Diplomatic missions of Afghanistan
Government of Mongolia
Government of Iceland
Emperor Haile Selassie I of Ethiopia
President Arbenz of Guatemala
President Iskander Mirza of Pakistan
Diplomatic missions of Turkey
Khodja, Minister of Agriculture, Syria
City of Moscow - 800 year anniversary since
   its foundation

RIO - 9900/9000 P.O. SET

King Mohamed Zahir Shah of Afghanistan

SPLENDID - 10160 O.P. SET

Queen Elizabeth II of Great Britain
President Paasikivi of Finland
King Mohammed V of Marocco
King Alphonso XIII of Spain
King Fuad of Egypt
Maharajah of Tripur
Maharajah of Hyderabad
Premier Hansen of Denmark
Government of Pakistan
King Faisal of Saudi Arabia
Lady Mountbatten
Gonzales Blanco, Minister of Labour of Mexico

MARIA THERESIA - 10620 SET   Ministry of Foreign Affairs of Czechoslovakia
Ministry of Foreign Affairs of Germany

POPE - 11520 SET   Pope Pius XI
Government of Eire
Embassy of Indonesia, London

ADELE MELIKOFF - 12940 O.P. SET   Shah Mohamed Reza Pahlavi of Iran
King Faruk of Egypt
President of Lebanon
Embassy of Pakistan, Washington
King Ammanullah of Afghanistan
President of El Salvador
Maharajah of Travancore
President Rene Coty of France
Gonzales Blanco, Minister of Labour of Mexico
Diplomatic missions of Iran

THOMAS - 14000 SET   Government of Nepal
Maharajah of Rampur

LADY HAMILTON - 15000 SET   King Mohammed V of Marocco
Maharajah of Travancore
Shah Mohamed Reza Pahlavi of Iran
President of Chile

MILADY - 15100 SET   Maharajah of Hyderabad

OLD FASHIONED - 15760 SET   United Nations Organization (UNO)

ARGENTINA - 16400 SET   Diplomatic missions of Argentina
Crown Prince Asfa Wossen of Ethiopia

NAPOLEON - 19720 P.O. SET   Embassy of France in Prague
Maharajah Surrendra Singh of Allrajpour
Archbishop Makarios, President of Cyprus

(This list furnished by Glassexport, PRAHA-LIBEREL-CZECHOSLOVAKIA.)

Ludvik or Ludwig Moser 1833-1916

From the 14th Century, small Bohemian towns were gradually making their glassware known throughout the world. By 1790 the glass manufactured in Bohemia had captured much of Venice's former glass trade. Its similarities to Venetian, German and Byzantine glass were quite remarkable.

The quality of the glass was achieved through many resources found in nature. Excellent fine white sand (quartz crystal) was in abundance. Large stands of beech trees provided fuel for the furnaces and ashes (potash flux) necessary to give their flint glass a quality resonance. Flint glass possessing a green hue was clarified by adding iron oxide prevalent in the sand. This resulted in a brilliant crystal which was as fine as real quartz crystal. Also, located on the outskirts of Karlsbad, Austria were vast quantities of uranium that had been accumulating for centuries. In 1853, by experimentation and trial and error, it was discovered that adding uranium oxides to glass could greatly alter its properties. This proved very advantageous, opening up a whole new field of manufacturing. A fluorescence, an almost luminous glow, could be achieved along with a yellowish green coloration. Some examples reveal an opalescence.

Other vast mineral deposits within the mountains aided in creating a spectrum of colors, encompassing noble (dark red), dark ruby, amethyst mauve, cobalt blue, topaz (smokey yellow), emerald green and cranberry. Moser's cranberry is undoubtedly one of the finest made as a result of large amounts of gold added to the batch.

Young glass artists were encouraged to create by the authority of the Austro-Hungarian Governments, which included Austria and Bohemia. It is not surprising then that Ludvik Moser excelled in a number of glass making aspects over most other artists.

MOSER The Great Glass Artist

In the workshop of the great artist O.J. Mattoni, as a student of his, the youthful Moser served his apprenticeship and learned the meaning of artistic value and sense.

Dr. Jean DeCarro found that the waters of the Health Spa at Karlsbad had healing powers, and because of this, established a permanent residency there with a Clinic. The Spa guests became a captive audience for the young glass artist, Moser, who produced glasses for drinking the water.

Tens of thousands of people each year visited the Spa, coming from all parts of the world, hence there was a market for artistic glass. The young glass artists would travel to the Spa and set up makeshift stalls and engrave or decorate the glass.

Because the young artist Ludvik Moser excelled in popularity and demand for his decoration, he was able to erect a shop of his own at Karlsbad in 1857. Ludvik Moser not only could create this glass in form and decoration, he possessed a lot of showmanship and strayed from the old concepts of shops and selling. In contrast of the area shops which were small, dark and dismal looking, Moser in 1857 erected a studio known as 'U mesta Vymaru (By the town of Weimar) on the street called Castle Hill, main street of Karlsbad. The walls were of cut mirrors, reflecting the beauty of his tremendous efforts in glass. He used large cut glass chandeliers which sparkled and twinkled as stars in the night. His showcases were of cut crystal, housing precious glass and also showing its reflections.

Moser established another studio in 1862 called U Zlateho klice (The Golden Key), on Mill Street. This shop featured cut mirrors and artistic glass products. In 1865 Moser opened his third studio on the Old Meadow known as U cerveneho sidce (The Red Heart).

The majority of the visitors who frequented the Spa were of the elite social groups, including sovereigns and statesmen. The stay sometimes became a bore at the Spa so here again Moser's wits came into action.

With the permission of the hotel and innkeepers, Moser organized a daily tour of his glass works. A huge luxurious sample room was filled with Artistic Glass that could be purchased. Needless to say, it sold well. Another idea of Moser's was allowing these customers, if they so desired, to blow a piece of glass. For the individual to take the blow pipe in hand and blow a piece of glass creatively was a special joy. Among those who blew their own piece of glass were King Edward VII, the Shah of Persia, the King of Siam, the Maharajah of Hyderabad and Travancore and many other persons of stature. Among those ordering glass was King Edward VII and his wife Queen Alexandria, Norwegian King Haakon VII, and Turkish Sultan Abdul Hamid.

Showrooms of Moser's glass were established at two other Spas, Marienbad and Franzenbad, and also a large studio in Prague. In addition to these studios, of which the one on Castle Hill was the most prominent, Moser also exploited his glass and new developments and forms in exhibitions. A recent find shows that he had a salesroom in Paris, also.

Thus the popularity of the man and his glass could do nothing but go upward. Yes, there was a charisma about Moser and it still lingers in his glass.

Whereas many of the factories of that era concentrated on mass production, Moser concentrated on individuality and glass was produced for the sake of art and art alone.

Moser enjoyed great success in the production of Artistic Glass until the time of his death in 1916.

EXHIBITIONS
(Ausstellung)

The exhibitions at which Moser exhibited and won honors were:
1869 - Austrian Museum for Art and Cewerbe in Vienna
1873 - Viennese World Fair.
1879 - Industrial Fair in Teplice.
1884 - New Orleans (USA).
1889 - Ausstellung in Frankreich.
1891 - Internationale Ausstellung in Tasmania.
1891 - International Ausstellung of Jamaica.
1892 - International Ausstellung in Columbia.
1892 - Ausstellung auf der Insel Man.
1897 - International Ausstellung in Brussels.
1905 - Ausstellung in Belgien.
1904 - World Exhibition in St. Louis (USA).
1900 - World Exhibition in Paris (silver Medal).
1906 - International Ausstellung in Mailand.
1910 - Ausstellung in Belgien.
1915 - International Ausstellung in San Francisco.
1921 - International Ausstellung in California.

SIGNATURES

Small script - etched, believed to be gold filled originally.
Large script - both etched and written in gold leaf, Moser-Karlsbad.
Moser - large block letters in gold leaf.
Moser - small block letters in gold leaf.
Moser factory stamp - round with M & M, Moser and Meyers.
Round paper label - Ludwig Moser Carlsbad in black letters.
Cameo cut back - in his rare Cameo glass.
Moser Karlsbad, Czechoslovakia - etched (the sons).
Oval yellow paper label - Moser Made in Czechoslovakia.
Oval acid stamp.

Names Given to the Tableware Service
For Various Heads of State

Splendid

The Czechoslovakian president gave this service as a wedding present to the Princess, now Queen Elizabeth II.

Those also ordering this service are:
Spanish King Alphonse XIII, at the time richest man in the world.
Nizam von Haidarabad
Maharajah of Triput
Maroccan King Mohammed the V
President of Finland
Minister President of Saudi Arabia
Government of Pakistan

Maria Theresia

This service was designed to honor the Queen Maria Theresia and the Kaiser. A very unique item, it was most expensive to produce with a Baroqian of a figural. A few pieces of this service are still on exhibit in the section of Schloss, at the Castle of Schonbrunn.

Maharani

This service was named because it was designed for several Maharajas of India. Among those the service was produced for were:
Maharaja Surrendra Singh of Ali Raipur
Maroccan King Mohammed V
Social Republic of Romania
Sonja Henie - On a visit to Czechoslovakia, ice skating and movie star

Sonja Henie chose this service.

Mozart

This service was very popular with artists and musicians - especially elegant.

Royal

At the beginning of the century, this table service was created for the Prince of Wales, later King Edward VII of England. He ordered one for himself and for his wife Queen Alexandra. It was known as the King Service. This service also decorated the tables of King Haakon VII of Norway, Turkish Sultan, Abjul Hamid and Turkish President, Celal Bayar.

The Pope's Service

This service was developed for all the Papal vessels of Pope Pius XI. Moser found a goblet of this design in a Parisian Museum that was made for the wife of Napoleon Bonoparte, Josephine Beauharnals. It contained six smooth sides known as the Schleifen. These vessels are still on exhibit at the Vatican and can be viewed by the admiring public.

Adele Melikoff

This is a variation of the Pope's service. This service was first ordered by a Princess of the Russian Court. The service was also ordered by the following:
Shah of Persia

Egyptian King Faruk
President of Lebanon
President of San Salvador
The Afghan King
Maharaja from Travancore
and many others
The above shows that many believed that
Ludvik Moser was capable of producing the greatest clarity and pureness in glass, for his great skill in creating these patterns and above all that he had great ability to please.

These great Heads of State must have vied for his commissions. Only he could fulfill them!

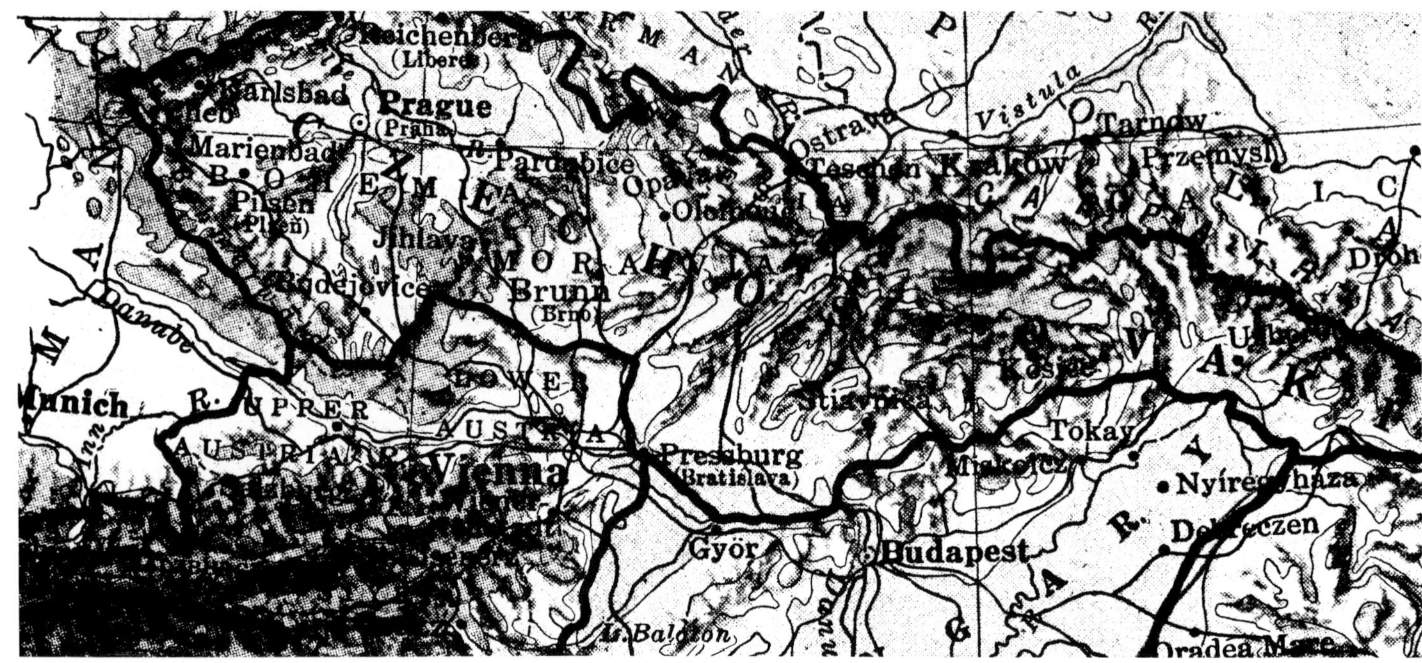

These two maps show the Bohemian area which was part of Austro-Hungary before World War I. In this 1919 map, above, Karlsbad is shown in the newly formed State of Czechoslovakia. This is where Moser opened his first glass house in 1857. Other studios or showrooms were in Marienbad, Franzenbad, Prague and in Paris. Note that the 1984 map, below, shows Karlsbad by its present name of Karlovy Vary.

THE BEGINNING OF THE FINAL END OF THE GREAT MOSER FACTORY UNDER THE DIRECTION OF THE SONS OF LUDVIK MOSER

Under the ownership of the father Ludvik, the Moser Glass Works became a world attraction. The trademark of "Moser" was rightfully called the "Glass of Kings". This was suddenly interrupted by the events of the great First World War. In 1916, Ludvik Moser, founder of this famous factory, died.

The two sons of Ludvik, Leo and Richard, who were well taught in the formulas of the glass and all the decorations used on it, carried on as owners of the firm. They had worked as salesmen for their father, so knowledge of promotion of the glass was not new to them.

After the First World War in 1918, an independent Czechoslovak Republic was established making a great political and geographical change. A great political and financial upheaval caught up the sons of Moser. They were forced to merge with the glass works of Meyer's Nephews of D Vary.

In his factory, Ludvik had previously employed many artists and engravers from this same factory. This newly formed company was called Moser-Meyer's Nephews Glassworks and was completely under the financial influence of the Bohemian Union Bank. A much larger enterprise resulted from this merger.

It resulted in the employing of the most skilled glass blowers, artists, technicians, decorators, chemists - the number of which exceeded a thousand.

The high quality of glass that Ludvik Moser was known for was upheld and his varied decorations on glass were repeated many times.

With the combined knowledge of these great artisans, shades of glass were developed never before known to man. Such was the result of this merger. Colors such as royalit (dark red), beryl (cobalt shading to turquoise), eldor (lemon yellow), heliolith (rich golden amber), and alexandrite (bluish purple coloration). It was the color alexandrite that put the glass makers of this famous glass works ahead of all other glass makers at the time.

The merging of these two famous companies allowed them to continue to supply their fine line of merchandise to the Royal Heads of State. They continued in the production of cognac sets, tableware, exotic vases, etc.

For the first time Moser's glass also was exported. The United States was a destination of this glass. It is estimated that at least three million dollars worth of the glass was imported for artistic value by the United States. For some strange reason, much of it went in the southern part of the U.S.A.

The great Depression of 1929 was worldwide and by 1932, the financial crisis was more than the Moser-Meyer's Nephews Glassworks could stand. The crash left the value of its stocks reduced to 20% of the original value.

By 1933 the Glassworks was finally sold in desperation. The last of the direct descendants, Leo Moser, son of Ludvik, lost his interest in the firm plus all his personal property.

The Moser Glassworks under Ludvik Moser was actively producing for 60 years followed by two years under the two sons of Moser and fourteen years under the merger of the two firms as Moser-Meyers Nephews.

Leo took a position as display manager with the Inwald Glassworks. During the Nazi occupation which began in 1938, Leo fled the country to save his life. The entire work force of this famous factory including the glass blowers, artists, engravers, and chemists were sent to concentration camps. It is very probable that most of these highly skilled and gifted men died there. A bitter end to one of the greatest glass making industries in history.

Leo Moser, who fled the country at the time of the Nazi invasion, made his escape to the United States, migrating to the Corning area in New York State and he settled there. He had high hopes of being employed in artistic glass work. Corning Glass was not producing art in glass at this time, but producing colorless glass for utilitarian purposes only. His aspirations of once again producing artistic glass were gone. Leo died in the United States. (See the story of his death.)

A large museum, housing Ludvik Moser glass in tribute to him and his successors, now stands in Karlovy Vary. This museum also contains a photograph of the original shop and one can see why it was superior to other shops at the Spa. Also in the Karlovy Museum is a letter being preserved addressed to Moser by the director of the Museum of Art and Industry in Vienna. This letter confirms that ''Mr. Ludvik Moser, industrial glass maker of Karlovy Vary'', published in 1880 and written by a Dr. E. Hlavcek, lists the name of the firm of Ludvik Moser informing the readers that Moser's glass had received many honorable prizes at a number of exhibitions.

As one sees the magnificent beauty of Moser's glass on display, it is very easily understood that under his scrutiny, the glass he produced was put through a series of twelve tests before acceptance.

After World War II, the glass works factory was completely demolished and in a desolate state. A factory was rebuilt upon the original site and has been operated under Communist government control since 1945.

Ironically, it has been given the name of Moser. This factory must not be confused with the one originated by Ludvik Moser and its production has none of the artistry or quality of the original Moser factory.

The glass being currently produced has an acid factory stamp as a signature.

Illustrated here is an example of a signature for the Moser and Meyers Nephews combine while Karlsbad was still located in Austria. The period of the combine was when the largest production came from the large glass works.

Moser Glass Today

Thanks to an export corporation called Glass - Export of Prague, not only royalty, but all who love the beauty of glass can still obtain that beauty produced by the Czechoslovakian glass makers. The Glass - Export firm made it possible to renew relations with famous customers, for heads of state to fill out their exquisite collection of drinking sets, etc. and also made it possible to buy in occupied Czechoslovakia.

Today as yesterday, Czechoslovakian or Bohemian glass means richly, cut crystal, two color engraved glass, sparkling chandeliers of crystal, and thin blown goblets.

The third largest industry in Czechoslovakia is glass making. This glass is exported to over one hundred countries. Also, today as yesterday, the government of Czechoslovakia trains high school students in three special glass making schools.

In Prague and Bratislava are art academies teaching young artists in glass to create, design and hand shape objects of art.

Among the young artists today at the Moser factory is Oldrich Lipa, designer; and Lubas Metelak, creative artist and engraver.

As one artist put it, "art exists only because someone cared enough to make it better than average." The beautiful artistic glass of Czechoslovakia bears this out. Even so, none of the present day glass can compare with the beauty produced by the master, Ludvik Moser.

Leo Moser's Death

The article below appeared in the *Collectors News*, Grundy Center, Iowa dated January, 1975. It is reproduced in its original form and serves as a fitting tribute to Leo Moser and the greatness of Moser Art Glass.

GRANDSON OF MOSER
GLASS FOUNDER DIES

Information has been received by Collectors News of the death in late November of Leo Moser, grandson of the founder of the famous Moser Glass Works, at the age of 95. He was buried Dec. 1st.

The company was founded in the late 1850s in Carlsbad, which is now Karlovy Vary in Czechoslovakia. It gained fame for the high quality of fine artistic glass as well as its tableware services for the crowned heads of Europe. Original pieces of Moser sell for prices up to $750.

Leo Moser had not been active in the company since the country was taken over by the communists after World War II. The firm still uses the Moser name and makes beautiful glass but, in the opinion of experts, it is not of the caliber of the old Moser pieces.

A Moser collector in the U.S. commenting on the death of Leo Moser declared, "He has left the world a legacy of beauty and the Moser name as maker of !the glass of Kings! never will die."

Herrn
John C. Mareska
2213 Cherry street
Toledo
Ohio 43508

PRAHA DNE 10.3.1981
ČÍSLO JEDNACÍ odb. II/Ad /316/81/

VĚC

Sehr geehrter Herr Mareska,

Herr Direktor Dr. Kuba hat Ihr Brief an das Kunstgewerbemuseum
in Prag übergeben und ich werde versuchen, einige Ihre Fragen
über die Glasfabrik Moser in Karlovy Vary zu beantworten.
Über Moser Glasfabrik existiert keine umfangreichere mono-
graphische Bearbeitung. Die wichtigsten Informationen über
die Familie und das Unternehmen finden sie in dem Artikel
in der Zeitschrift Czechoslowak Glasreview, welche sehr wahr-
schreilich in der Bibliothek des Corning Glassmuseums zu
haben ist /Jindřich Hájek, Karlovy Vary, The Cradle of the
Glass of Kings. Glasreview 19, 1964, pp.43 ff./ In diesem
Jahr (1981) erscheint in dieser Zeitschrift auch eine um-
fagreichere Studie über Moser-Glasfabrik, ich werde Ihnen
diese Nummer, als sie erscheint, gleich schicken.
Eine sehr detailierte Bibliographie über Moser ist zusammen-
getragen in dem ausgezeichnetem Buch "Sammlung Karl H.
Bröhan - Berlin. - Kunsthandwerk - Glas, Holz, Keramik",
Berlin /West/1976/. Verfasst von K. Bröhan/. Wenn diese für
Sie unerreichbar ist, kann ich Ihnen eine xeroxkopie von
Seiten über Moser schicken.
Man weiss zwar, dass Ludvik Moser ein ausgelernter Graveur
war, aber es sind keine eigenhändigen Stücke von ihm bekannt-
nur einige Gläser, an denen die Karlsbader Graveure wie Hoffmann
oder Urban oder Urban beteiligt waren . Die Produktion nach
1893, als Moser eigene Glashütte gebaut hat, ist in Haupt-
zügen bekannt, leider ist aber das Archiv der Firma nur sehr
lückenhalf erhalten.
Ich selbst plane während dieses diesen Sommers eine Studie
über Moser zu schreiben - die aber an die Stilenticklung der
Produktion zwischen 1900-1938 konzentriert ist, und befasst
sich nur sehr wenig mit der Historie der Firma. Wahrscheinlich
im Herbst könnte ich Ihnen mehr Informationen über Thema-
Moser schreiben.

Dr. Alena Adlerová

*This letter in the Czech language was received by Dr. John Mareska who has worked closely with Mrs.
Charon on the study of Moser . . The letter is from the Museum at Prague and answers questions about
Moser and his glass.*

Vases by Moser

Moser expressed his great talents in his variety of vases whether they were miniatures to contain violets or large vases to hold florals. These are found many times in matching pairs to grace a mantle, adorn a stairway, hall or the balconies of the homes and castles of the families of royal blood.

The vases shown in the following plates are fine examples of this quality of glass with unrivaled decorative qualities. One can easily visualize these same vases with mirrors behind them and understand why Moser won international fame.

Plate 1

Plate #1, 4 and 5

This large, 20-3/4 inches in height vase of the richest of cranberry color is one of a kind and is beautiful almost beyond description. There are twelve water birds in flight of rich enamels from base to rim of this vase. Birds fly from swampland, tree stumps and wood florals. The rare, large handles are entirely covered in a gold leaf and vine decoration in tapestry fashion.

Plate 4

Plate #7, 9 and 10

Large bulbous vase is of a very deep cobalt color with a window pane effect throughout the vase. Decor illustrating a large enameled chicken is in an attack position after a snake. It is Arabic in motif.

A large ribbon brocade effect enriches the vase giving the color of the chicken much more effect. The same enameled brocade enhances the base of the bulbous vase. Throughout the vase are large florals with outlines of gold leaf making a very impressive pattern.

Plate 9

Plate 10

This rare raisin colored vase is an overall height of 7 inches. It has four snail like feet applied with all over encrustation in gold ribbed fashion. It is decorated in an all over off white with grape leaves and vines twining in and out of clusters of grapes. Gold leaf adorns the outlines of the grapes, leaves and vines.

Plate #13 and 14

This is a rich moss green vase in cylinder shape. The motif of tall grasses comes from the base of the vase and extends to the rim of the vase. A applied glass parrot is perched on a large stalk and is decorated and enameled in brilliant hues of red. Feathers of the parrot are etched into realistic shadings. This is a good example of Moser's applied glass on glass artistic motif sculptured into realism.

Plate #15

This is another example of Moser's applied glass showing his glass artistry. On this heavy cut diagonal vase, the glass is shaped to give a three dimensional effect.

The turkey motif is applied on a cut vase with shading from clear into tones of amethyst. It is a wooded scene of trees, rocks and grasses found near a body of water seen in the background. A large, wild male turkey is found in the tree and two wild hen turkeys on the ground. It is a remarkable picture of wild life. The vase is 7 inches in height and 8-1/2 inches in width.

Plate #16, 17 and 22

This extremely fine, heavy crystal vase is 14 inches in height, classical in shaping and the motif is in Moser's Marquetry or Padding. The Christmas cactus is of brilliant red and with deep intaglio or engraving found in the large buds of cactus and leaves. Pieces with Moser's Marquetry are very, very rare.

Plate 22

Plate 17

Plate #23, 24, 25, 25A

This is a cylinder shaped, cut crystal vase for which Moser chose the theme of the "Three Muses", depicting the stages of life. The Muses are on applied 3-1/2 inch cobalt colored medallions. The Women are extremely well done in enamel and are very realistic. It has gold leaf on the rim and base and small gold leaf leaves, pods, and berries encircling the panels on the vases which is 12-1/2 inches in height.

Plate 25A

25

This is a rare example of Moser's Cameo in glass in a rich golden amber coloration. Seven recessed lines are carved and gold filled with 24K gold leaf on this 15 inch vase. In a chipped ice acid finish are carved elephants of various sizes and poses in a tropical scene of palm tree and bush. The elephants are gold leafed on this vase. You will find "Moser Karlsbad" in the cameo cutting. The goldsmith initials "K" are signed. Only on important pieces of glass was the goldsmith allowed to sign. The vases of this caliber were invariably only for exhibition.

Plate #33

This vase has a very majestic look to it. It is completely covered in a variety of designs, one intermingling into the next. Lifelike leaves are within a white background and florals are within medallions. There are vines and sprigs in gold leafing. The closeup shows the extreme beauty and detail in Moser's decorations. This vase is accented by four amber feet and the serrated or pointed rim is of the same rich color.

Plate #37

A small 4 inch vase which shows the beauty of simplicity. It is built on four applied button like feet. The squatty vase is of a very light smoke color. It has a simple decoration of a large Carp among reeds or rushes in water. The fins, lips and gills are decorated with extreme beauty. Water lily and weeds in water are found on the other side of the vase. A beautiful rolled rim and applied snail handles accent its simplicity.

Plate #41, 42, 43

   *This pair of matching rich cranberry vases is pro-
portioned for use on a mantle. These vases have large
gold leaf strawberries and leaf design and trailing
vines in gold leaf. Moser again shows his talent for
portrait painting on large applied medallions. These
two women are very true to life and attired ex-
travagantly in dress and hair fashions of that period.
Note the love knots of florals placed in their hair,
their necklaces and their life like hands. The skin
tones are of true color. The shape of the vases,
although large, are still daintily formed to compliment
the portraits.*

Plate 43
Close up

Close up
Plate 42

Plate #44 and 45

Moser's use of blue glass and his derivatives of that color was an achievement in itself. In this large 15-1/2 inch electric blue vase, he demonstrates this ability. It has the shape of a narrow vase at the rim, widening in the center and has a pedestal style base. This vase features, among the tree branches, apple blossoms in bloom, a male exotic bird on one side of the vase and a female exotic bird on the other side of the vase. The shadings and colorations of the birds are extremely well done.

Plate 45

These miniature vases of unusual shape illustrate the two motifs that Moser was famous for. They are identical in shape and of rich cranberry color. One miniature depicts his famous applied glass grapes and grape leaf decor. Matching is the blue miniature in his famous applied acorn and oak leaf motif. The acorns and grapes were decorated and then the leaves were gold leafed. One of the vases still contains the original paper label (Plate 48) "Moser Karlsbad Austria". Vases also are signed in block letters of gold leaf and numbered. These vases are very rare.

Plate 46

Plate 48

31

Plate 48A

Plate 49

Plate #51

   This large, 10 inch, bulbous vase has the amberina coloration and thumbprint form. Moser's amberina was and is rated among the finest. The rich amber shades delicately into rich cranberry coloration. The vase is completely decorated in a large fall leaf with various shades of blues, white and an almost orange color. There is gold leaf and enameled vines throughout the leaves and a small round berry on the vines.

A nautical scene on sea green cut crystal decorates this 7 inch bulbous vase which is exceptional in the deep engraving of the marine life. In the deep engraving, a winged sea fish is swimming toward the surface. Air bubbles of various sizes bring the fish alive. It has very deep engravings of swirls, cut to clear, creating sculptured waves and the tail of the fish is in action. The other side shows an identical fish in a downward swim. The bubbles of air, the tail is swishing in the opposite direction and again it has sculptured waves. The fish is an acid finish in relief with gold leaf sea weed around the base of the vase. The top of the vase is a cut serrated swirl of gold leaf.

Plate #54

This is one of the finest examples of Moser's engraving on glass in a rare color of amethyst. The walls of this thick cut vase had the amethyst coloration blown within a clear glass outer layer. A large engraved tulip adorns this vase and is typical of Moser's engraving. The decor of leaves and stems in bent form flows around the complete vessel.

Prominent Artists

Moser employed some of the greatest engravers and artists. Among them were Edward Hoffmann and his son, Johann. This father and son team was known for its engravings and figural scenes. Josef Urban and his son, Julius were prominent. Rudolf Hiller, who was known for his historical characters and hunting scenes, was well known.

Wines

In Austria, in that region called Bohemia, was located one of the greatest areas for the growing of grapes. Therefore, much wine was produced in this area.

In all probability one of the forms that Moser produced the most of was glasses for drinking wine, such as:

— Tasters or snifters to test the wine.
— Wines with open stems allowing the toasting to be done on either end.
— Wines used at the October-Fest Celebration of the Grape and the wine.
— The Romer stem was very prevalent. This stem was also produced in the German regions. Many times the Romer stem was accented by gold leafing.
— Slender petite stems, hollow blown cylinder shaped and then decorated.
— Punts or berry like applications of glass applied to the stem to prevent the hand from slipping. Many times the stems were accented by intaglio cutting and then gold filled.
— The early air-twist stem was used with a different color used in the air-twist.
— Cut stems, flared stems and, many times, elaborate florals.
— Portraits, glass in the form of jewels, acorns, and grapes were incorporated.

Ludvik Moser developed as much imagination and artistry in the stems of his wines as in the cups of these drinking vessels.

The cups of his stemware were highly decorated in costly shaded enamels, florals accented by silver and gold applications. These cups many times resemble a flower and your imagination may lead you to believe it was opening up to the sun. Like so many artists of the day, Moser's art in glass was in accord with nature.

His range of variances was in form, style, color, and height. These decorations were the greatest in his development of champagnes, wines, cognac, brandy and other glasses.

Almost all of the wines produced by Moser were blown in one piece, a tremendous feat in itself.

The cups of his wines were shaded many times. He had the uncanny ability to shade from one color to another and defy the human eye to determine where one shade stopped and another began. He shaded from clear to various colors of green, amethyst, cranberry, and ruby.

A commemorative wine decorated with shamrocks in celebration of St. Patricks Day. Rich grass green is used for coloration and the shamrocks are beautifully done in a darker green in the wine cup. Circling in garland drape fashion is a beading of reddish enamels. The stem has five romer type rings and the base flares slightly to enhance the small shamrocks.

Plate #61 and 62

One of Moser's famous designs, almost a trademark of his, is the all over leaf and fern design. It is all over green glass with leaves done in rich and costly shades of enamels and 24K gold leaf is used to accent the outlines of the fern. There are small puff florals of various colors found throughout the design. This stem is completely enameled and gold leafed. The same design is carried onto the base. It is 6-1/2 inches in height.

Plate #63 and 64

A development in design attributed to Moser was his famous acorn and oak leaf. It is shown on the richest of cranberry coloration. The cup of this wine is fused to glass acorns, then decorated into realism and the oak leaves are decorated in enamels and gold leafing. There are acorns and leaves trailing down a plain open stem and the base has matching decor with the cup. It is more of a chalice than a wine.

Plate #65, 66, 67

The most difficult colors to achieve in glass are those in the rainbow. On this cup of inverted thumb-print design is found three colors of the rainbow, yellow, blue and pink. On the cup an engraved or intaglio floral is placed and then filled in with 24K gold leaf accented by gold leaf trailings. A double notch is used on the stem with punts to prevent slipping when the goblet is held. To avoid the appearance of being overdone or letting the cup remain the outstanding feature, a plain flared romer stem is used. This item is very rare.

Plate 69

Plate #68 and 69

Very little has been found or recorded about the Padding or Marquetry done by Moser. When it is found, it rates as the finest done by any of the great glass artists of the day. On this wine are clusters of grapes of extreme beauty and well done, with trailing vines and a floral in rich amberina coloration. Within the flowers is an accent of dark shading. The entire decor of Moser's Marquetry is classical in shape. The cup is done in richly brilliant glass with a thin cut stem. The same theme is carried out on the underside of the base.

Plate #70, 71, 72

Engraving of immense beauty is the floral on this wine. The close up shows stemens and brush like engraved features. Only Moser was capable of trailings around the rim of a wine. The cup is done in shading of light green to the top and around the top of the cup. It has intaglio and filled in closed buds and leaves. The cup is set in a stem almost like the form of a flower and is regal in shape. It has a stem that is engraved and the underside of the base is in the same engraving. Plate #71 shows the monogram on the wine glass. A similar monogram was made for the Moroccan Sultan Sidi Mohamed. It was shown in the Czechoslovakia Glass Review in 1964.

Close up
Plate 71

Plate #74, 75, 76, 77, 78

One of the most beautiful and intricate designs is shown here. In an almost fan like form is an encrustation of gold leaf design on a melon shaped cup. The rim of the wine is done in rare scalloping. The stem is hollow blown and the fan like scroll is applied half way down the stem. Plate #77 shows the tremendous beauty of the all over decorated base. The wine itself is in shadings of clear to light greens in color.

Close up
Plate 76

Catastrophe!
Plate 78

Close up
Plate 80

Plate #79, 80 , 81

This wine can be rated as one of Moser's most decorative. Completely covering the wine is an all over fern decoration in enamels and gold leaf. White enameled dots, often found on Moser's glass, highlights the rim of the wine. The open stem, embellished with large berry like punts, is heavily encrustated with gold. The base is highly decorated with fluting and in between each fluting is another embellishment of gold leaf. The wine color shades from clear into blues. The shading is reversed in the stem and base.

Plate #82 and 83

This section on wines warrants another example of Moser's early intaglio or engraving which captures a slight illusion of amethyst coloration in brilliant glass devoid of any other color. The floral engraving is highlighted by the simple form of this wine. A slight engraving on the foot of the wine is to give balance to the floral engraving on the cup. It shows Moser's purity and clarity of glass which was dazzling. His glass surpassed the German "Wald Glas" and also the glass produced in Venice, Italy at the time.

Plate #85 and 86

This spectacular wine is done in light coloration of clear to green. A band of 24K gold leaf is applied to the cup. The band is done in a scribble design with jewels fused onto the glass in between the designs. This is another application often found in Moser's glass. It has an air-twist stem of cylinder shape with two knobs near the foot of the wine and the same decor of gold leafing and fused jewels carried on the base. It is a majestic wine indeed.

Juice Glasses

The juice glass is another form that Moser produced. They are desirable and collectible. As the wines, champagnes, etc. were produced for the drinking of wine, the juice glasses were produced for drinking grape juice.

Some were produced to be part of a table setting. Most of the glassmakers of Europe produced thirteen as a set whereas the Americans marketed twelve.

Many pieces were produced one of a kind for special occasions or especially for some one person. Juices also were produced in matching pairs. The glasses were often decorated as a commemorative to a town, place, person, or an occasion and were often dated. The size of the juice glass was invariably the standard size of 4 inches.

Ludvik Moser and his sons, Richard and Leo, were so diversified in their developments, designs and forms that one could collect their glass exclusively and have hundreds of pieces each different from the next. The plates used in this book show that diversity.

The table settings, including the juice glasses, were never considered common place. As much artistry was applied to these as to any other form. Thus, all juice glasses the Mosers produced were objects of art. They are still available and can be found by the collector today.

The following examples of Moser's glass used for juice exemplifies to what extent he could decorate on what other artists may term insignificant pieces.

Plate #88 and 89

This piece has coloration from clear into slight amethyst shadings. It has a gold leaf rim and white enameled scrolls done in a V fashion. The reverse is found on the base of the glass. Within the scrolls, three red jewels are fused onto the glass and filigree scrolls of gold leaf embellish the glass. White beading typical of Moser's glass is found beneath the rim. On the base of the juice in Plate 89, is found one of the signatures used! **"Glassfabrique"** *M & M, a picture of a wine glass and* **Moser, Karlsbad, Austria.** *The signature was used after the merging of Moser's Sons and Meyers Nephews Glassworks in 1921. Ludvik Moser, the father, at one time hired many of the glass experts from the Meyer's Nephews factory. After the merger, the artistic glass continued to be produced.*

Plate 89
Detail

Plate #90 and 91

   An all over decoration was lavishly given to this juice glass. On rich emerald green color, a 24K gold leaf band was applied to the back, rim, and base of the glass. Within the gold leafing, a decorative scroll and beading follows the gold leaf. Fern and vine decoration are on the body of the glass, then panels of applied glass beads enhance the glass immensely.

Plate #92 and 93

This juice is found with an all over decor-ation. Glass beading called corolene is of the finest crystal glass fused onto the vessel. On the rim of this glass is found large grape leaves. From the vines, clus-ters of grapes hang in a realistic manner. Coloration of the glass itself is very rare. In a very pale, almost amberina shade blended to a slightly smokey color, it makes a rare combination of colors. Plate #93 shows a close up of leaves, vines and grapes. The intricacy of the vines, in the leaves and detailed perfection of the grapes is superb.

Plate #94 and 95

"Resplendence in color" could be the term for the decoration of this juice glass and matching champagne. It is ornamented with an all over encrustation of 24K gold leaf and then a design is done in a freize style within gold leaf. A sort of "window pane" treatment is incorporated which allows the rich cranberry color to emerge. Within the panes of color, a small, shield like decoration is used. It is a truly regal piece.

Plate #96

The florals, violets, are so realistic one can almost pick them off the glass. On deep emerald green, the violets surround the top of the glass and trailing vines, leaves and buds seem to be three dimensional. The rim of the juice has a large band of gold leafing and a design within that band. It gives contrast to the richness of the rest of the juice glass.

This glass is classical in shape and uses the Lily of the Valley decor, a petite decoration used many times by Moser. Lily of the Valley is decorated on a wide band of gold leafing extending from the rim to the base of the glass. Moser did not apply the gold leaf panels on his works in a straight fashion, but always applied it in a circular movement giving a free form feeling. The glass is green in color and the remainder of the glass is decorated in gold leaf, fernery, and florals. Plate #98 is a close up of rich gold leaf band and Lily of the Valley floral.

Plate #99 and 99A

This beautiful, rich green decorated piece is set in a highly decorative metal holder. It is decorated in petite florals, clusters of grapes, grape leaves and vines in gold leaf. It has an applied, wide gold leaf band to the rim of glass. The holder is highly polished metal. The twisted handle and decor is in grape leaves to correspond with decor of the glass. The close up of this glass shows the uncanny beauty of a combination of metal and glass. It is a commemorative piece.

Plate 99A

Plate #100, 101, 102

This glass warrants three plates to show the detail of Moser's engraving on glass. This is a fine example of an engraving of a building on rich cranberry glass. The extreme detail in his windows, the outline of the building and chimneys is almost three dimensional. The other side of the glass is done in simplicity on a large area of gold leaf, trailing vines and grapes. Plate #102 displays the detail of Moser's work in his leaf decoration. The rim is done in slight gold leaf and gold leaf outlines the plaque of the buildings.

Plate 101

Plate #104 and 105

This is another perfect example of the design developed by Moser with the leaf and vine. The large leaves are done in shaded quality enamels of different colors. The outline of leaves and vines is accented in gold leaf. Note the extremely lifelike beauty of his butterfly amidst the leaves. It has an all over decoration and yet does not have an overdone look, something only Moser was capable of doing. It has a light greenish color in the glass.

Plate #106, 107, 107A

Only Moser could apply a large, brilliantly enamel-ed flower on each side of this juice and not have it look out of proportion to the rest of the decoration. It is decorated in various shades of blues, whites and reds, with flowers of petite size with filigree of gold leaf encircling them. The blue color of the juice shows through to accent the brilliance of the large flowers.

Group of glasses
Plate 107A

Unusual Drinking Vessels

Ludvik Moser always remained the artist. Much like the American born artist, Louis Comfort Tiffany, Moser could capture more colors of the rainbow and produce more movement in form than any of his counterparts of that day.

His greatest endeavor, from the time he was a young student, was to produce something other than commonplace glass.

Moser was a pioneer with his application of gold and silver leaf, and enamels of the costliest. Many times the design was engraved and then filled in. Because of this talent and his originality of design, it is little wonder that he excelled over all other artists of that period to be commissioned in 1870 to the Imperial Court of Franz Joseph, House of Hapsburg, ruling power at that time over Austria.

This fact was documented by an article written by Dr. E. Hlavek in 1880 and an advertisement in a publication "A Guide to Karlovy Vary".

From that time on, he became a commissioned man to all the Royal Heads of Europe for their glassware. He was given the title "Supplier to the Courts of the Royal Crowns of Europe and Their Dignitaries".

Moser's name stood foremost for the highest quality, uniqueness in form and originality in crystal glass design. Moser led the way by upholding the best traditions of Czech glass making.

The tradition of Moser's great work was carried on by his two sons after his death in 1916. Ludvik taught his sons the art of his decoration and instilled into them the importance of the production of quality glass. For this reason the great artistic glass continued to be produced after his death.

The following unusual drinking vessels are examples of his ability for uniqueness and artistic design:

Plate #108

This chalice is a tremendous display of reality of the figures of the deer. The stag is in various poses in a forest setting. The hunting scene is a cameo cut back technique appearing like chipped ice, making a winter scene possible. This piece dates in the very early 1850's. It is 11-1/2 inches in height and was used as a commemorative piece or a drinking vessel presented at the festivities for toasting. It is very rich, early Bohemian red color. The chalice has a very unusual cutting on the foot and base.

Plate #109, 110, 112

This is an example of the fantasies that Moser was capable of producing. The vessel is done in highly decorative, colored florals, scrolls with a shield and a coat of arms. It is embellished in different brilliant enamels and gold leafing. The handles are in the form of the Phoenix bird, and are applied and gilded heavily with an encrustation of 24K gold. A very fine threading of glass is applied about three inches from the rim of the vessel. A pearlized effect is given to the sides of the object. The coloration is of very rich golden amber.

Plate 110

Plate #113 and 114

   This shows a saddle on stirrup glass lavishly decorated in an all over encrustation of gold leaf. Petite florals in shaded enamels complete a very desirable motif. Highlighting the decoration is a large sunburst and within the sunburst are enamels, swirls and dots. It is a very rare piece and is 4-3/4 inches high.

Plate #116, 118, 119

This handled cup is decorated entirely of nature's decor. Applied beetles are enameled in realistic colors to the cup. The body of the cup is a crackle glass giving the illusion of the beetles being captured in a web. Large green glass leaves and branches are applied. The handle is entirely of gold leaf like the base of the cup, which is heavily gold leafed, giving the impression of being a tree and tree trunk. An unusual green smoke color is given to the cup.

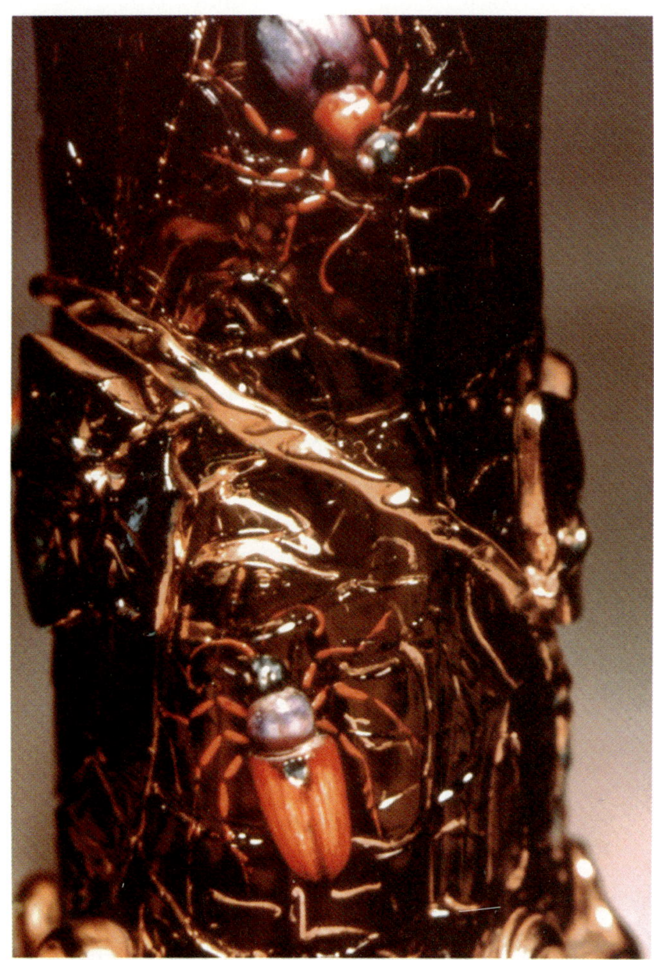

Plate 118
Close up Detail

Close up
Plate 119

Plate #120 and 121

A very unusual shape of a hunting vessel in the form of a horn of plenty. The horn of plenty is applied to a standard making it an all over height of 9-1/4 inches. The body of the horn of plenty is a very rich cranberry color and is decorated in gold leaf flowers and tendrils flowing down the body. The standard is of colorless glass with a motif gracing it. The top of the horn is accented with rich gold leafing. It was a presentation piece to a sportsman.

Plate #123 and 124

These hunting vessels of identical shape are very rare, not only in form, but decoration as well. In the shape of a horn, they have applied handles which made it easy for hunters to carry.

In a light green coloration, Plate 124 shows an interesting scene of a hunter on bended knee with his gun. The dog beside him is on the alert for the prey. The remainder of the vessel is decorated in gold leaf acorns and oak leaves showing a fall scene. The handle is beautifully applied.

Plate 123 also was used in hunting. It is horn shaped and is a beautiful cobalt color. The glass cut to clear is extremely well done and rare. The applied handle is decorated with a white enamel design and has heavily applied white enamel also decorating the main body. The enamels are outlined by gold leafing.

66

One of the most classical in shape with an almost cylindrical form. This elongated cup is for toasting with wines. It is cranberry color in a very rich hue and it has a beautiful application of a twisted and decorated handle. A close up of the cup shows wide bands, large leaves, and a series of leaves on the front of the cup are all elaborately decorated with corolene beads. It is highly embellished with gold leaf. An attractive chain like decor is found within one band and jewels are speckled on each leaf. Small flowers enhance the remainder of the cup with leaves and branches being used intermittently. It has an applied decorated handle.

Plate 130

Plate 131

Detail
Plate 132

Plate #135, 137, 140

The three handled Loving Cup was used often as a Presentation Cup in European countries. It also was called an Award Cup. It was given for advancement in the army, or as appreciation for a duty well done. This cup was always looked upon in a favorable way.

The cup is cranberry color and the applied handles are in colorless glass so they will not detract from the cup itself. Plate 140 shows a close up of the cup. You can see the extreme beauty of the decoration with small flowers in pink and blue shading. It has a swag like design within a shield shaped decoration. Note the white beading within the shield.

Detail
Plate 140

70

This very unusual drinking vessel of extreme beauty is almost like a pilsener glass with a handle. It is completely covered with gold leafing. Small florals are located beneath the rim of the cup. A band two-thirds of the way down from the rim and florals incorporated within the band make a majestic motif. The base is decorated in the same fashion with shaded florals. A completely gold leafed thorn handle puts the finishing touch to this extremely ornate piece.

Close up
Plate 143

Plate #144 and 144A

This large Romer is one of the finest examples of Moser's famous grape and grape leaf decoration. On a rich sea green color, he has completely covered the cup of the vessel with applied glass grapes of blue, red, and green colors and they were then gold leafed. Intertwining with the grapes are leaves in shaded colors. Beetles in three forms of flight are found within the grape vines and leaves. The same decor is carried on the large hollow stem and base. Gold leaf punts are used and the finishing touch to this magnificent object is the rim and the base in gold leaf. The height is 10 inches. It was used at the October-Fest.

By adding a thin layer of gold leaf to his enamels, Moser was able to subdue all of his colors, thereby, eliminating garishness or an overdone look.

This Chapter is of Great Historical Value

Plate #145, 145B, 145C, 145D

An awesome vase but it is also a fearsome painting, on colorless glass. It is a painting of the "Berghof", home of Adolph Hitler.

It was identified from the book "Hitler - the Pictorial Documentary of His Life" by John Toland.

The picture shows the "Berghof" exterior (evidently it was built as early as 1924 as the caption states).

Toland writes that, the traditional pitched roof design was part of his (Hitlers) architectural credo: "The house with the flat roof" he wrote in 1924, "is Oriental - Oriental is Jewish, Jewish is bolshevistic."!

The "Berghof" is believed to have been built by the great architect Albert Spears. The "Berghof" was located at the southeast tip of German Bavaria, south of Salzburg.

The vase depicts the mountain slope in the narrow Ache Valley of the scenic Bavarian Alps overlooking Austria.

The "Berghof" was a rambling two story building. In one room, was a huge picture window 25 ft. by 12 ft. which commanded a magnificent view of the Alps. It was reportedly in front of this window that Hitler stood for hours receiving inspiration for his grandiose schemes.

The "Berghof" was connected by an intricate maze of corridors and rooms which were carved out of solid rock inside the mountain on the slope where the chalet was built.

From the chalet an elevator ascended more than 300 ft. to the "Eagles Nest", Hitler's personal retreat. The "Berghof" was bombed in World War II by the British Royal Air Force who dropped 6 tons of bombs on it and the barracks of the S.S. (Elite Guard) April 25, 1945.

"Eagles Nest" was captured May 3, 1945, by the troops of the United States Third Division. Presently, an "Eagles Nest" replacement still stands as an historic site for tourists and serves as a restaurant.

The vase is signed in silver script, "Moser".

Plate 145

No doubt the painting on the vase was a forced commission at the time of the Nazi invasion in 1933 or thereabout. Proof of that is the location of the Nazi flag flying in the breeze on the vase. Probably under protest, it is barely painted inside the vase structure.

Data on the "Berghof" is taken from Colliers Encyclopedia Volume 3. The Swastika was adopted in 1920 as the symbol of the National Socialist Party in Germany.

In a previous chapter, I have written that the entire work force, giants of the trade who devoted their whole life to the making of artistic glass, were committed to the Concentration Camps in 1933.

From the book "Adolph Hitler" by John Toland, we learn that Hitler had great aspirations to become an artist. In 1907 he made an attempt to enroll in the Academy of Fine Arts in Vienna. He failed the examination, but according to a Professor Hitschel of the University, Hitler's paintings did show a remarkable architectural precision. He was more architect than painter. Hitler took another examination in October, 1908 and failed again.

Thus, probably because of his love for architectural subjects, we have this great painting of the "Berghof" on glass. The original "Berghof", now destroyed, still remains in memory on this glass vase.

Detail
Plate 145D

Plate 145C
Reversed, enlarged

Plate #147, 149

Another great example of Moser's capability to paint subjects on glass is this one of a beautiful semi-nude woman. We usually associate his work with his great artistic designs gold leafing and carving on objects with a purpose in life such as his wines, cognac sets, drinking vessels, tableware, etc.

Portrayed here is a tremendous example of his ability to paint portraits or figurals on glass. It is an art form equal to any painting on canvas.

The coloration of her skin tones are true to life. The gracefulness of her pose is classical. The close up shows brush strokes and detail in the facial features. When you turn this plate around, the beautiful woman changes poses.

The plate is signed in gold leafing with block letters, ''Moser'' and numbered.

76

Plate #150A and 151A

This unusual decanter has color similar to celedon. It has applied glass grapes and highly enameled leaves and trailing vines.

Detail
Plate 151A

Plate #154, 155, 156, 157

   In a rich, decorated cranberry color this decanter set is shown with 8 liquors, all within a glass the shape of an egg. It is upheld by three brass legs and is very rare.

Plate 157

Plate 156

Plate #159, 161, 162

   This jewelry box is in a highly enameled decor of florals and leaves with an unusual brown color. Birds are shown in various poses on each side of the box.

Detail
Plate 160

Detail
Plate 161

Plate #163 and 164

This decanter depicts a man and woman on a horse.

Detail
Plate 164

This is a boula bowl with decor of Moser's fantasy glass, using mythical characters in song and dance. The cover and standard is of polished brass.

Detail
Plate 169

Plate #170 and 171

This saddle glass has decor with a knight in armor. It has an all over leaf and vine decoration.

Plate #172

    This triangular footed bowl is decorated in highly enameled leaves.

Plate #173, 173A, 174

    These matching pouring vessels and the handled vase are made in celedon like glass. They are highly decorated and enameled with applied jewels fused on- to the glass. It is very rare.

Plate 173A

Plate 174

87

Plate #175 and 176

This round hinged box is of deep cranberry color with highly enameled Lily of the Valley decor.

Plate 176

Plate #177 and 178

A large colorful applied bird is sitting on branches within the enameled leaves and vines. Moser's famous ribbed snail feet adorn this vase.

*Detail
Plate 178*

Detail
Plate 180

Plate #182 and 183

This pedestaled decanter set is in rich emerald green. It has acorn and oak leaf decorations.

Plate #181

This covered large Romer drinking vessel depicts a knight in armor.

Plate #184

This handled drinking vessel is ornamented with a tropical bird in vivid colors.

This is a fantasy done on a decanter with a falcon hunting bird.

Plate #186

93

This cup and saucer is in opaline glass with decor of a cherub in bright enamels.

Plate 188

Plate #189 and 191

Decorated in his very rare cameo technique with brown coloration and a signature worked into the cameo.

Plate 191

95

A NEW ACQUISITION

Plates 207, 208, 209, 210, 211, 212, 213

This new acquisition is well worth photographing
and including in this book.

This five-piece dresser set was produced in the
deepest of cranberry coloration. The decor is applied
and includes large and small acorns with trailing vines
and leaves. The color is labeled as Venetian Rose.

The original label on the large decanter reads as
follows:

No. 4368 Verre 8' ean
Bouigises 6 pr. V'enit rose, g, blanc
Deca: 45©44.40 Carafe 9, 45
Cacalon 5, ko, Sverier gt, gobel 7.95
Plateau 12,60

The original label is a silk ribbon signed as follows:
Cristallerie De Karlsbad
Ludwig Moser & Fils
24 Boulevard Des Italiens 24
Paris

Plate 208

Plate 209

Plate 210
Detail

Detail
Plate 211

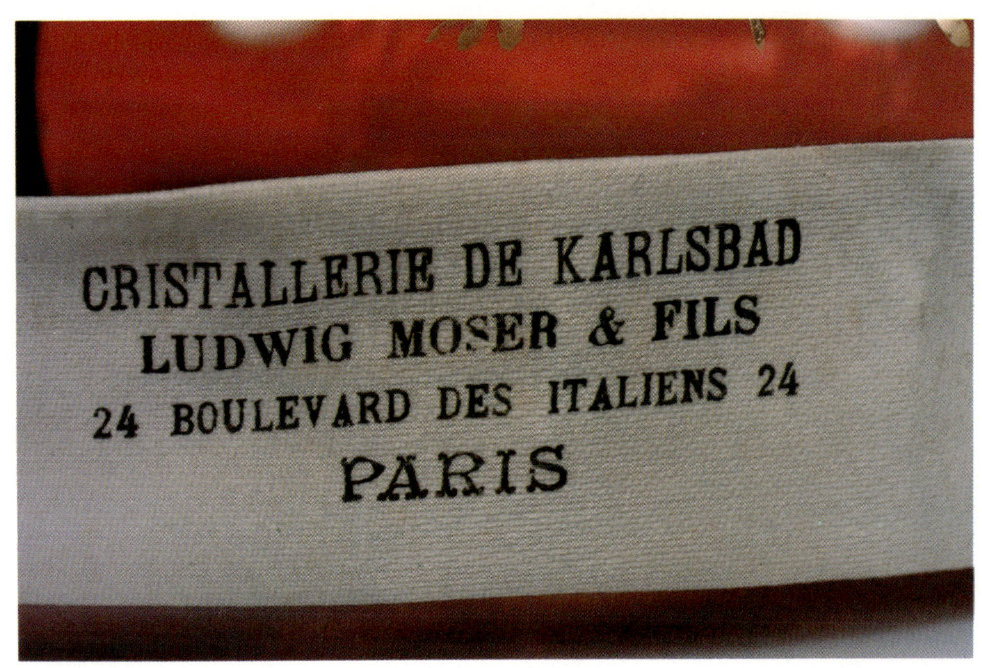

Plate 212
Detail

Closeup
Plate 213

99

Plate 194

Plate 195

100

Plate 196

Plate 198

Plate 199

Plate 200

Plate 201

Plate 202

Plate 203

104

Plate 204

Plate 205

Plate 214

Plate 215

Plate 216

Plate 190

107

Plate 136

Plate 139

108

Plate 56A

Plate 119

Plate 134
Detail

Detail
Plate 148

BIBLIOGRAPHY

Advertisement - Moser Bohemian Crystal Witness of History, Glass Export, Praha - Liberec - Czechoslovakia.

Benezit, E. *Dictionnaire des Peintres, Sculpteurs, Dessinateurs et Graveurs*. France: Librairie Grund, 1960.

"Bohemian Glass," *Hobbies*, Volume 79 (December 1973),

"Glass," *Encyclopedia Britannica* (1954 ed.) Volume 10,

"Grandson of Moser Glass Founder Dies, *"Collectors News"*. (January 1975).

Hajek, Jindrich. "Karlovy Vary - the Cradle of the Glass of Kings," *Glass Review* Volume 19 (1964).

Homlyn, Paul. *Bohemian Engraved Glass*. Prague: Knigtisk, 1968.

Mackay, James. *Turn-of-the Century Antiques* New York: E.P. Dutton and Company, Incorporated, 1974.

McKinley, Gawain. "Lotz and Austrian Glass," *Discovering Antiques*. Volume 14, pp. 1721-1724, New York: Greystone Press, 1973.

Middlemas, Keith. "Glass from Bohemia," *Discovering Antiques*. Volume 14 pp. 1712-1735, New York: Greystone Press, 1973.

Nejdl, K. *Ludvik Moser's Historical Development*. Karlovy Vary-Dvory: National Corporation, 1962.

"Project Design of Glassworks in Czechoslovakia," *Glass Review*. Volume 23 (1968).

The Random House Collector's Encyclopedia Victoriana to Art Deco. New York: Random House, 1974.

Wilson, Peter (ed.) *Antiques International,* New York: G.P. Putnam's Sons, 1967.